WESTERN CHRISTIANITY NEVER BEEN PURE

A Treatise

CHARLES MWEWA

Copyright © 2024 Charles Mwewa

www.charlesmwewa.com

Published by:

ACP

Ottawa, ON Canada

www.acpress.ca

www.springopus.com

Email:

info@acpress.ca

All rights reserved.

ISBN: 978-1-998788-69-9

DEDICATION

To

The purest form of Christianity,
To the glory of God.

CONTENTS

DEDICATION iii
CONTENTS v
BRIEF INTRODUCTION vii
1 | VINDICTIVENISTIC CHRISTIANITY 1
    Period 1
    Characteristics 1
    Key Impurities: 2
    Conclusion 3
2 | INDULGENISTIC CHRISTIANITY 5
    Period 5
    Characteristics 5
    Key Impurities 7
    Conclusion 8
3 | IMPERIALISTIC CHRISTIANITY 9
    Period 9
    Characteristics 9
    Key Impurities 11
    Conclusion 12
4 | MATERIALISTIC CHRISTIANITY 15

Period 15
Characteristics 15
Key Impurities 17
Conclusion 18
5 | VOLUMINISTIC CHRISTIANITY 19
Period 19
Characteristics 19
Key Impurities 21
Conclusion 22
ABOUT THE AUTHOR 23
SELECTED BOOKS BY THIS AUTHOR 25
INDEX 31

BRIEF INTRODUCTION

Christianity is a pure and honest religion, but Western Christianity has never been pure. This is a historical fact. Apostle Paul of Tarsus, strove to take a pure form of Christianity to Europe, but he confronted a world filled with doctrinal confusion. There, he encountered demonic religious, unknown gods, philosophical stray dogs, and a place unable to comprehend the pure grace of God without human engineering.

Christian pioneers faced a harsh political environment in Europe. The first missionaries were captured, imprisoned, persecuted, prosecuted, and killed. This, too, is a historical fact. Europe was averse to pure Christianity from the beginning. Even when Christianity was finally received, it was diluted with political hard talk, economic imperialism, social superiority, religious sophistication, mental animistic, and moral incongruency.

This trend has not ended; it only, like matter, only changes states. Between the 2nd Century and the 1300s, Western Christianity was vindictive; between the 1400s and the 1600s, it was indulgenistic; between the 1600s and the

1900s, it was imperialistic; between the early 1900s to the late 1980s, it was materialistic; and post-1980s to the present, it is voluministic.

Thus, Western Christianity has never been pure.

It was this very impure form of Christianity that was imported to the Americas, and from the Americas, to the rest of the world. The tenets of pure religion are enshrined in these words of the Apostle James:

> Do not merely listen to the word, and so deceive yourselves. Do what it says. .
> Anyone who listens to the word but does not do what it says is like a man who looks at his face in a mirror and, after looking at himself, goes away and immediately forgets what he looks like. But the man who looks intently into the perfect law that gives freedom, and continues to do this, not forgetting what he has heard, but doing it--he will be blessed in what he does. If anyone considers himself religious and yet does not keep a tight rein on his tongue, he deceives himself and his religion is worthless. Religion that God our Father accepts as pure and faultless is this: to look after orphans and widows in their distress and to keep oneself from being polluted by the world.[1]

---

[1] James 1:23-27

In brief, pure religion, and by extension pure Christianity, has the following tenets:

1. It does what the Word of God says;
2. It frees (freedom);
3. It has moral integrity and accrues dignity;
4. It considers the interests of the vulnerable first; and
5. It is not corrupt nor does it transact in corruption.

The Christianity of many non-Western countries may be purer than that of Western countries. As will be suggested in this book, Western Christianity has transacted in bondage and not freedom, dependence and not independence, cultural antagonism and not cultural integration, conceptualization of incomplete humanity and not full sense of humanity, especially for those lands which were colonized, and engineered charity and not pure love.

Simplicity is the cure for the impurities of Western Christianity. In the West presently, the impure type of Christianity it had embraced for centuries is waning. Even mega churches are losing masses. People are shunning reading the Bible, and majority of the young and modern generations are questioning beliefs which their ancestors had held dear. This is, partly, because they can see the hypocrisies of their ancestors who practiced racism, bigotry, slavery and colonial repression while they still claimed to be decent Judeo-Christians.

The gist of this treatise is to persuade all men and women to return to pure Christianity, not Western Christianity. The Apostolic generation was challenged by its Lord when He insisted that they took the Gospel to the Gentiles. Some of the Jewish leaders resisted, but others like Paul, became an Apostle of grace to the Gentiles. The type of Christianity that Paul promulgated, began to be diluted and to die slowly across the ages. Love started to be replaced by greed and the wanton disregard for the plight of the poor, the widows, and the marginalized of this world.

1 | VINDICTIVENISTIC CHRISTIANITY

Period

Between 2nd Century and the 1300s

Characteristics

The early Apostles of Christ had long gone. In place of pure Christianity, heretic dogmas saturated realms and the scholastics. These trends are historical facts. During this period, Europe persecuted the Church, and derogated from the pure form of Christianity.

This era includes the Ante-Nicene period

(100 to 300 AD), the First Seven Ecumenical Councils (300 to 700 AD), and the Middle Ages (800 to 1200 AD). This era, too, is the beginning of the Renaissance. While, the Renaissance is the awakening of scholastic and thought, it was also an atrocious era that militated against pure Christianity.

By the 1300s, European Christianity was dominated by Catholicism. Historic orders, including the Benedictines, Cistercians, and Premonstratensians, collectively known as the monastic orders, dominated the Western Christian religion in Europe. They were joined by the Mendicant orders. These began to realize that the Christianity of the first century had been neglected. So, they demanded that Christianity begin to focus on poverty, and pastoral ministry, or a return to caring ministry as the early Apostles of Christ were instructed.

Key Impurities:

- Christianity did not do what the Word of God says.
- Christianity did not or rather, had neglected the plight of the vulnerable.

Conclusion

Even with this impure form of Christianity, lacking in the pure application of the Word of God, God was still working in human affairs through His grace. Pure Christianity seeks to do what the Word of God says, and not merely stating its precepts. Pure Christianity, similarly, must target the poor, the widows, and all the marginalized and vulnerable people.

2 | INDULGENISTIC CHRISTIANITY

Period

Between the 1400s and the 1600s

Characteristics

This period is the late Middle Ages to the Early Modern Period in Western Christendom. This era is at the height of heresy and schism. There were massive divisions among religious fraternities to the point of blood. In this period, the City of Constantinople fell to Ottoman.

That in historical parlance, simply meant the fall of Christianity and the emergency of Islam.

The Byzantine Empire was conquered in 1453, and the entire Orthodox communion of the Balkans and the Near East sided with the powerful Ottoman Empire. Islam would impose its culture and religion across most of Eastern Europe, and the moral decline in Western Europe became a norm.

The Catholic Church began to sell indulgencies, relics of certain Christianity icons. This period was showcasing a Christianity that was cold and was selling salvation. Until Martin Luther confronted the Catholic Church and with it the emergency of Protestantism, Western Christianity was in a vicious state of corruption.

In this period, powerful emperors in Europe were sending Christian missionaries across the world to look for new territories to conquer, mostly in the pretext of spreading the Word of God. Slave trade is at its peak and only Whites were truly people; all other races of humanity were only firewood for hell. Christianity in Europe was in such a state of corruption, bigotry and divisiveness that the distinction between religion and politics had become thinner and non-existent.

The papacy was domineering, even in control of vast territories of Europe. European kings and emperors subscribed in ideas and thought to the corrupt papal state. Indulgencies, thus, thrived at the guise of self-enrichment. During this period, which we may term, para-imperialistic, the world was questioning the authority of the Word of God. Men, rather than God, became heaven's final arbiters, claiming to have the power to release people's souls from purgatory by the purchase of relics. Spiritual authority now rested in the hands of heavily corrupt men who loved themselves more than God, and a Christianity corrupt by personal aggrandizement.

This type of Christianity was being transported overseas and in time, it would lead to one of the worst imperial avarices of the ages, colonialism

Key Impurities

- Christianity neglected to do what the Word of God says;
- It had curtailed freedom;
- It had lost moral integrity and it shunned the dignity of other races of people;

- It did not just neglect the interests of the vulnerable, it also took advantage of their vulnerability for its own gain; and
- It was corrupt at the core.

Conclusion

This historic 200-year period is *anathema* in history, especially, in the sane history of human dignity. It was a bridge from worse to worst in human treatment and dignity. Europe was at this time using Christianity, and by extension, the free grace of God for its own selfish interests. The foundation for moral, spiritual, cultural and political corruption of the world, was set in this period. From this epoch, Western Christianity would become a weapon for brutal enslavement, corruption, and colonialism.

But it was also a period in which God was working through a select few men to challenge the corrupt Roman papal church and to spread the Word of God by the printing of Bibles. The Reformation was birthed during this period.

3 | IMPERIALISTIC CHRISTIANITY

Period

End of the 1600s to the end of the 1900s

Characteristics

This is the most hypocritical era of Western Christianity. Energized by the Industrial Revolution, and the transfer of power from the bishopric to emperors, Western Christianity was, in this period, in a state of acquisition.

Capitalism, *per capita* income, and improved

standards of living and massive investments in industries rather than in agriculture, brought in an existence unequaled in economic terms in history. Better standards of living also meant that people's life expectancies went up and there was minimized infant mortality rates.

However, what was happening economically did not translate into divine or spiritual integrity. Greed among major Western countries gripped princes, kings and emperors. That was the official birth of imperialism. A British queen called Victoria inspired grand imperialism – the acquisition of faraway lands and territories and many empires in Europe followed suit.

By 1885, major Western countries had congressed in Berlin, Germany and divided Africa as a source of raw materials to feed the mega industries in those countries. It was acquisition at all cost – guns, pens and Bibles played the same role, grab everything that had value, including human life.

Christianity was now a weapon of mass destruction. In one voice, Western imperialists preached the love of God, and in the other, the love of money. It was an instance of serving two masters at the same time.

The Berlin Congress ushered in colonialism,

and the disregard for human dignity and respect. Acquired lands were forced to convert to Western Christianity, replacing their cultures (names, standards, edifices, etc.) and dismissing them as of no moral or civilized value. The gods of other lands became demons, but even the God they replaced such gods with, was a superiority God, who only considered Whites from Europe and America as humans, and all others as mere accidents of nature.

Thus, this era was the heightening of racism, bigotry and marginalization of peoples, tribes and races. A Gospel Minister would preach from the Bible love, and from the Bible justify slavery and serfdom; he would preach a one God who made all creatures equal, and from the same Bible justify segregation, Apartheid, xenophobia, and hate.

Key Impurities

- Christianity neglected to do what the Word of God says;
- It had curtailed freedom so much so that it became an instrument of Satan;
- It had lost moral integrity and it shunned the dignity of other races of people, to the extent that it sold and

traded in human slaves as merchandise;
- It did not just neglect the interests of the vulnerable, it also took advantage of their vulnerability for its own gain; and
- It was corrupt at the core, and introduced the vice of corruption in the other continents, especially in Africa.

Conclusion

Forced Christianity was corrupt. It was a weapon of colonization. It ensured that the conquered territories were indoctrinated into what was considered standard and ideal in Western Europe, using the Bible. This kind of Christianity was grossly impure and mechanistic. It was a murderous Christianity – it buried everything in its way, cultures, traditions, folklores of other people, etc. It killed self-expression and relegated the conquered groups into oblivion. It paved the way for materialism and grand corruption. It is responsible for the moral decay of the world today.

However, God is gracious, using the same corrupt, imperial Western Christianity, God has reached to many lands and these lands have begun to return to the Scriptures by themselves.

They do not need to be taught what the meaning of Scripture is, they can see for themselves and receive balanced and holistic revelation that do not discriminate, marginalize and relegate others in second-class creatures. Even with this plus, imperialistic Christianity was still beyond the pale.

4 | MATERIALISTIC CHRISTIANITY

Period

End of the 1920s to the 1980s

Characteristics

By the end of the 1980s, most Western imperial powers had almost lost their overseas colonies due to independence. To their credit, they had already amassed wealth from these territories, and now, it was time to enjoy their accruements.

What was obtaining in the social, economic

and political world, was also happening in the religious world. Churches and ministries in Western countries started to emphasize material prosperity as a standard of spirituality. This was an oxymoron as the nations they had formerly colonized were left with dysfunctional structures and governments. It would set a trend in economic and religious terms of mass begging (donations) and confusion all across the globe.

Thus, Western Christianity could depend on the wealth it had grabbed from the vanquished territories, but what would the converted in formerly colonized countries depend on? The reinstitution of slave-master relationships began to show up in religious, political and economic relationships.

For example, in Catholicism, the papacy still controlled the thought of the world. One single message was designed from Rome, and all adherents were to follow that each Sunday, without any exception. This was not different from the older ages in which the papacy fed its adherents with replica indulgencies. Western Christianity via the Vatican City still imposes its Western-centric religion on other lands and continents. When babies are baptized, they are christened with Western names, exactly as those lands, had lost their authentic cultures and ways of life through imperial colonialism.

And in the Protectant movement and circles, Western Christianity still calls the shots. The songs churches sing in other parts of the world, are mainly composed by Western Christians, and even the commentaries Gospel Ministers emulate in other parts of the world, are Western-centric. In many of these fraternities, spiritual precedents are still set by Western Christians, such as revival pioneers, religious cultural influencers, expressions, dressing, and types and sounds of music. There is little of other people's originality left in the world. What Western Christianity says is the truth, others take it as truth, and vice versa.

The materialistic movement is being challenged. However, spirituality still remains tied to how many cars, houses, dress suits, and travel itineraries one Gospel Minister has over another.

Key Impurities

- Christianity did not just neglect the interests of the vulnerable, it also boasted for having more than the marginalized and the poor could ever dream possible in their lifetime. The measure of success became how many basketfuls of offering were collected *per* Sunday.

Conclusion

God's grace has prevailed, even when the materialistic world has clawed into church pills and pulpits. Some prosperity preachers and influencers have fallen into scandals one after another, and the veil has been lifting. Slowly but surely, God is bringing His people back to pure Christianity, and many non-Christian organizations, ironically, have taken upon themselves to satisfy God's compassion by providing relief to the poor, the widows and the marginalized in the world.

5 | VOLUMINISTIC CHRISTIANITY

Period

From the 1990s to the 2000s

Characteristics

This epoch or era is characterized by volumes. There is a penchant and proclivity for voluminous services and masses, voluminous car parks, voluminous number of attendees, voluminous registration of new members, etc.

Indeed, historical Christianity values

additions and multiplications of the saints. That paradigm is still efficacious. However, Western Christianity's current view of growth is for the glory of men and not of God.

Each church or denomination or Gospel Minister may want to attribute growth to themselves – their intelligence, capabilities, talents and graces. God is left out of the equation. To some, smaller ministries and congregations are no longer fashionable. In some instances, they are even laughing stocks.

The elephant in the room is money. Volumes are being preferred because they bring in large sums of money through tithes and offering. It is not the purity of the Word of God or of Christianity that is motivating many; it is greed.

This era may trigger all the indignities which were prevalent in previous eras. In the name of church-growth or some other eschewed hypothesizing, many of the historical impurities may be finding their way back into the pure Body of Christ.

The injunction of Revelations is instructive in this era: "Nevertheless I have this against you, that you have left your first love. Remember therefore from where you have fallen; repent and do the first works, or else I will come to you quickly and remove your lampstand from its place—unless you repent."[2]

The idea of meganism sounds catchy and flashy, but actual critical review makes it look very atrocious and venomous. Such mega ministries or churches are actually competitive schemes in the guise of powerfulness. Only the mega preacher is the main beneficiary of the mega brand, and the majority may just be pawns in the religious chess game. Sometimes, even the Lord Jesus is only a means to the end, the end of which is to maganize the preacher and his mega brand.

In many of the mega congregations, individuality is sacrificed at the altar of corporateness. The individual, the soul for whom Jesus Christ our Lord shed His blood, may become just an insignificant tool for the grand glory of an organization or a person.

Key Impurities

- Christianity is neglecting to do what the Word of God says; it should return to love, especially to caring for the poor, widows, the marginalized, and the lost. That is true spirituality. And

---

[2] Revelations 2:1-7

- The knack for volumes sacrifices truth and pure Christianity for human attraction. Christianity must remember the words of its Lord and Founder, "For where two or three are gathered in my name, I am there…"[3] Intent, and not volumes must be the core value of Christianity in the present era.

Conclusion

God's grace is still overriding some people's craving for pageant and grandstanding. Through other modern platforms such as social media and others, God is still working in the lives of His little flock.

Indeed, mass gatherings, mass congregating and mass services and celebrations are a plus if the glory of God is the aim. For from such, there could also be mass and voluminous conversions. Other than that, a large political forum and event may have more value than a mega church gathering.

---

[3] Matthew 18:20

ABOUT THE AUTHOR

Award-Winning, Best-Selling Author, Charles Mwewa (LLB; BA Law; BA Ed; LLM), is a prolific researcher, poet, novelist, lawyer, law professor and Christian apologist and intercessor. Mwewa has written no less than 100 books and counting in every genre and has exhibited his works at prestigious expos like the Ottawa International Book Expo and is the winner of the Coppa Awards for his signature publication, *Zambia: Struggles of My People*.
Mwewa and his family live in the Canadian Capital City of Ottawa.

SELECTED BOOKS BY THIS AUTHOR

1. *ZAMBIA: Struggles of My People (First and Second Editions)*
2. *10 FINANCIAL & WEALTH ATTITUDES TO AVOID*
3. *10 STRATEGIES TO DEFEAT STRESS AND DEPRESSION: Creating an Internal Safeguard against Stress and Depression*
4. *100+ REASONS TO READ BOOKS*
5. *A CASE FOR AFRICA?S LIBERTY: The Synergistic Transformation of Africa and the West into First-World Partnerships*
6. *A PANDEMIC POETRY, COVID-19*
7. *ALLERGIC TO CORRUPTION: The Legacy of President Michael Sata of Zambia*
8. *BOOK ABOUT SOMETHING: On Ultimate Purpose*
9. *CAMPAIGN FOR AFRICA: A Provocative Crusade for the Economic and Humanitarian Decolonization of Africa*
10. *CHAMPIONS: Application of Common Sense and Biblical Motifs to Succeed in Both Worlds*
11. *CORONAVIRUS PRAYERS*
12. *HH IS THE RIGHT MAN FOR ZAMBIA: And Other Acclaimed Articles on Zambia and Africa*
13. *I BOW: 3500 Prayer Lines of Inspiration & Intercession from the Heart: Volume One*
14. *INTERUNIVERSALISM IN A NUTSHELL: For Iranian Refugee Claimants*
15. *LAW & GRACE: An Expository Study in the Rudiments of Sin and Truth*
16. *LAWS OF INFLUENCE: 7even Lessons in Transformational Leadership*
17. *LOVE IDEAS IN COVID PANDEMIC TIMES:*

For Couples & Lovers

18. *P.A.S.S: Version 2: Answer Bank*
19. *P.A.S.S.: Acing the Ontario Paralegal-Licensing Examination, Version 2*
20. *POETRY: The Best of Charles Mwewa*
21. *QUOT-EBOS: Essential. Barbs. Opinions. Sayings*
22. *REASONING WITH GOD IN PRAYER: Poetic Verses for Peace & Unconfronted Controversies*
23. *RESURRECTION: (A Spy in Hell Novel)*
24. *I DREAM OF AFRICA: Poetry of Post-Independence Africa, the Case of Zambia*
25. *SERMONS: Application of Legal Principles and Procedures in the Life and Ministry of Christ*
26. *SONG OF AN ALIEN: Over 130 Poems of Love, Romance, Passion, Politics, and Life in its Complexity*
27. *TEMPORARY RESIDENCE APPLICATION*
28. *THE GRACE DEVOTIONAL: Fifty-two Happy Weeks with God*
29. *THE SYSTEM: How Society Defines & Confines Us: A Worksheet*
30. *FAIRER THAN GRACE: My Deepest for His Highest*
31. *WEALTH THINKING: And the Concept of Capisolism*
32. *PRAYER: All Prayer Makes All Things Possible*
33. *PRAYER: All Prayer Makes All Things Possible, Answers*
34. *PRISONER OF GRACE: An I Saw Jesus at Milton Vision*
35. *PRAYERS OF OUR CHILDREN*
36. *TEN BASIC LESSONS IN PRAYER*
37. *VALLEY OF ROSES: City Called Beautiful*
38. *THE PATCH THEOREM: A Philosophy of Death, Life and Time*
39. *50 RULES OF POLITICS: A Rule Guide on Politics*
40. *ALLERGIC TO CORRUPTION: The Legacy of*

President Michael Sata of Zambia
41. INTRODUCTION TO ZAMBIAN ENVIRONMENTAL LEGISLATIVE SCHEME
42. REFUGEE PROTECTION IN CANADA: *For Iranian Christian Convert Claimants*
43. LAW & POVERTY *(unpublished manuscript)*
44. CHRISTIAN CONTROVERSIES: *Loving Homosexuals*
45. THINKING GOVERNMENT: *Principles & Predilections*
46. WHY MARRIED COUPLES LIE TO EACH OTHER: *A Treatise*
47. LOVE & FRIENDSHIP TIPS FOR GEN Z
48. POVERTY DISCOURSE: *Spiritual Imperative or Social Construct*
49. SEX BEFORE WEDDING: *The Tricky Trilemma*
50. QUOTABLE QUOTES EXCELLENCE, VOL. 1: *Knowledge & Secrets*
51. QUOTABLE QUOTES EXCELLENCE, VOL. 2: *Love & Relationships*
52. QUOTABLE QUOTES EXCELLENCE, VOL. 3: *Hope*
53. QUOTABLE QUOTES EXCELLENCE, VOL. 4: *Justice, Law & Morality*
54. QUOTABLE QUOTES EXCELLENCE, VOL. 5: *Dreams & Vision*
55. QUOTABLE QUOTES EXCELLENCE, VOL. 6: *Character & Perseverance*
56. QUOTABLE QUOTES EXCELLENCE, VOL. 7: *Actions*
57. QUOTABLE QUOTES EXCELLENCE, *1 of 20: Knowledge & Secrets*
58. QUOTABLE QUOTES EXCELLENCE, *2 of 20: Love & Relationships*
59. QUOTABLE QUOTES EXCELLENCE, *3 of 20: Hope*

60. *QUOTABLE QUOTES EXCELLENCE, 4 of 20: Justice, Law & Morality*
61. *QUOTABLE QUOTES EXCELLENCE, 5 of 20: Vision & Dreams*
62. *THE SEVEN LAWS OF LOVE*
63. *THE BURDEN OF ZAMBIA*
64. *BEMBA DYNASTY I (1 of a Trilogy)*
65. *BEMBA DYNASTY II (2 of a Trilogy)*
66. *ETHICAL MENTORSHIP: Missing Link in Transformational Leadership*
67. *AFRICA MUST BE DEVELOPED: Agenda for the 22nd Century Domination*
68. *INNOVATION: The Art of Starting Something New*
69. *TOWARDS TRUE ACHIEVEMENT: The Mundane & the Authentic*
70. *ONE WORLD UNDER PRAYER: For Camerron, Ecuador, and France*
71. *ONE WORLD UNDER PRAYER: For New Zealand, Poland, and Uganda*
72. *ONE WORLD UNDER PRAYER: For Malta, USA, and Zambia*
73. *ONE WORLD UNDER PRAYER: For Germany*
74. *ONE WORLD UNDER PRAYER: For Haiti, Iraq, and Russia*
75. *ONE WORLD UNDER PRAYER: For Chad, UN, and Syria*
76. *ONE WORLD UNDER PRAYER: For Burundi, Canada, and Israel*
77. *ONE WORLD UNDER PRAYER: For China, Egypt, and Venezuela*
78. *ONE WORLD UNDER PRAYER: For Greece, Mali, and Ukraine*
79. *ONE WORLD UNDER PRAYER: For Morocco, North Korea, and the UK*

80. ONE WORLD UNDER PRAYER: *For Belgium, Brazil, and the Burkina Faso*
81. ADIEU PERFECTIONS: *A Satire*
82. OPTIMIZATION: *Turning Low Moments into High Comments*
83. ACING THE IMPOSSIBLE: *Faith in the Other Dimension*
84. END GAME LAW: *Financial Mindset in Quotables*
85. MARRIAGE MAPPING METHODOLOGY: *The Outline of How to Measure the Strength, Love-Condition and Longevity of a Marriage*
86. A CASE AGAINST WAR: *The Imperative of Love and the Unsustainability of Peace*
87. BORROW TO GROW: *Accessing Other's Achievements to Your Benefit*
88. WESTERN CHRISTIANITY NEVER BEEN PURE: *A Treatise*
89. MISERABLE UNSAVING: *A Poetic Satire on Money Mindset for Non-Saving Upbringings*
90. SURVEILLANCE AND THE LAW: *The cases of Canada and Zambia*
91. TALENT: *The Unfair Principle of Fairness*
92. MORAL CAPTALISM: *The Critical Examination of the Concept of Rightness in the Context of Human Goodness*
93. MONEY: *All about the Exchange*
94. *A Job Called* MARRIAGE
95. HAGGLERS ASSASSINS: *Overthrow of the Malazonian Government*

INDEX

1

1300s, 1
1400s, 5
1600s, 5
1900s, 9
1920s, 15
1980s, 15
1990s, 19

2

2000s, 19
2nd Century, 1

A

acquisition, 9, 10
Africa, 10, 12, 25, 26
aggrandizement, 7
agriculture, 10
Americas. *See* Western Christianity
ancestors, x
Ante-Nicene, 1
Apostle James. *See* pure religion
Apostle Paul of Tarsus, vii
Apostolic generation, x
authority, 7
awakening. *See* Renaissance

B

babies, 16
Balkans, 6
baptized, 16
Benedictines, 2
Berlin, 10
Berlin Congress, 10
Bible, x, 11, 12
bigotry, x, 6, 11
Body of Christ, 20
bondage, ix
Byzantine Empire, 6

C

capabilities, 20
Capitalism, 9

Catholic Church, 6
Catholicism, 2, 16
celebrations, 22
Christendom, 5
Christian, 23
Christianity, iii, vii, viii,
    ix, x, 1, 2, 3, 6, 7, 8,
    9, 10, 11, 12, 16, 17,
    18, 19, 20, 21, 22
Cistercians, 2
colonialism, 7, 8, 10, 17
colonies, 15
colonization, 12
congregations, 20, 21
Constantinople, 5
continents, 12
corporateness, 21
corrupt, ix, 7, 8, 12
corruption, ix, 6, 8, 12
cultural antagonism, ix
cultural integration, ix
cultures, 11, 12, 17

D

dependence, ix
dignity, ix, 7, 8, 11
discriminate, 13

E

Early Modern Period, 5
economic imperialism.
    See Western
    Christianity
emperors, 6, 7, 9, 10
enslavement, 8
Europe. *See* Western
    Christianity

F

firewood, 6
First Seven Ecumenical
    Councils, 2
folklores, 12
freedom, viii, ix, 7, 11

G

Gentiles, x
Germany. *See* Berlin
glory, iii, 20, 21, 22
God, 26
Gospel Minister, 11
governments, 16
grace, vii, x, 3, 8, 18, 22
graces, 20

greed, x, 20
guns, 10

H

human life, 10
hypocrisies, x

I

imperialism, 10
imperialistic. *See* Western Christianity
impurities, ix, 20
incomplete humanity, ix
independence, ix, 15
individuality, 21
indoctrinated, 12
indulgencies, 6, 16
indulgenistic. *See* Western Christianity
Industrial Revolution, 9
infant mortality, 10
influencers, 17, 18
integrity, ix, 7, 10, 11
intelligence, 20
interests, 8
Islam, 6
itineraries, 17

J

Jewish leaders, x
Judeo-Christians, x

L

law, 23
lawyer, 23
Lord and Founder, 22
love of God, 10

M

marginalization, 11
marginalized, x, 3, 17, 18, 21
Martin Luther, 6
masses. *See* volumes
masters, 10
materialistic. *See* Western Christianity
materialistic movement, 17
materialistic world, 18
mega brand, 21
mega churches, ix
meganism, 21

mental animistic. *See* Western Christianity
Middle Ages, 2
missionaries, vii, 6
monastic orders, 2
money, 10, 20
moral decay, 12
moral incongruency. *See* Western Christianity
multiplications. *See* volumes

N

number of attendees. *See* volumes

O

originality, 17
Orthodox, 6
Ottoman, 5

P

papacy, 7, 8, 16
papal state, 7
pastoral ministry, 2
per capita income, 9
pioneers, vii, 17
poor, x, 3, 17, 18, 21
poverty, 2
Premonstratensians, 2
professor, 23
prosperity, 16, 18
Protectant, 17
Protestantism, 6
pure Christianity, vii, ix, x, 1, 2, 18, 22
pure religion, viii

R

races, 11
racism, x, 11
Reformation, 8
registration. *See* volumes
religious sophistication. *See* Western Christianity
Renaissance, 2
revival, 17
Rome, 16

S

Satan, 11

scholastic, 2
Scriptures, 12
second-class creatures, 13
self-enrichment, 7
self-expression, 12
selfish interests, 8
serfdom, 11
services. *See* volumes
Simplicity, ix
slavery, x, 11
smaller ministries, 20
social media, 22
social superiority. *See* Western Christianity
spirituality, 16, 17, 21
standards of living, 10
Struggles of My People, 23, 25
success, 18
Sunday, 16
superiority God, 11

T

talents, 20
tenets. *See* pure religion
territories, 6, 7, 10, 12, 15, 16
the West, 25
tithes and offering, 20
traditions, 12

V

Vatican City, 16
Victoria, 10
vindictive. *See* Western Christianity
volumes, 19
voluministic. *See* Western Christianity
vulnerability, 8, 12

W

wealth, 15, 16
weapon of mass destruction, 10
Western Christianity, vii
Western names, 16
Whites, 11
widows, viii, x, 3, 18, 21
Word of God, ix, 2, 3, 6, 7, 8, 11, 20, 21

Z

Zambia, 23, 25, 26, 27

www.ingramcontent.com/pod-product-compliance
Lightning Source LLC
Chambersburg PA
CBHW072040060426
42449CB00010BA/2369